SACRED STONES

The standing stones of West Wales;
their history and traditions

Terry John

GOMER

First impression—July 1994

ISBN 1 85902 127 1

© text, Terry John

© illustrations, Terry John

Printed by J.D. Lewis and Sons Ltd., Gomer Press, Llandysul

I am most grateful for all the help I have received during the writing of this book; in particular, I should like to thank Janet Bray, Jean Brown, Mary John, Andrew and Helen Kirkhouse, Alison Morris, Tim Painter, Nona Rees, Tony Roberts, the staffs of Haverfordwest Public Library and the Royal Commission for Ancient Monuments, Aberystwyth, and Dyfed Elis-Gruffydd and Mairwen Prys Jones of Gomer Press.

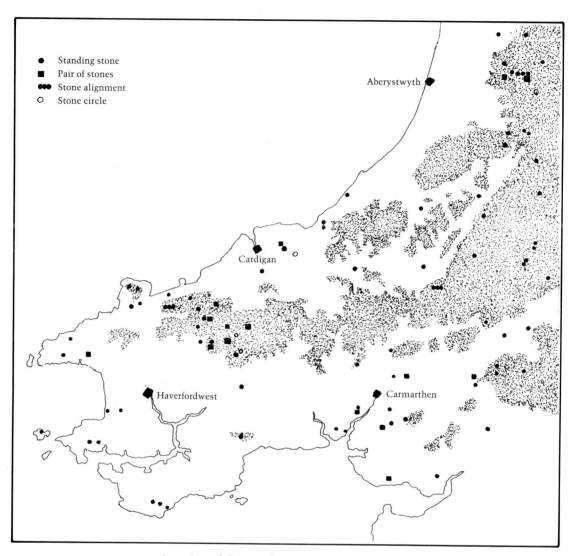

Location of the standing stones of West Wales

CONTENTS

INTRODUCTION

The Bedd Morus stone is a familiar sight to those who cross the mountain between Newport and the Gwaun Valley in Pembrokeshire; indeed, travellers on the narrow road might be forgiven for ignoring the stone, especially on a day of bright sunshine when the sky is vibrant with larks. Then the stone is only a small part of a wide and spectacular landscape, where low stone walls snake across the moorland and the surging heather is strewn with boulders.

Those who encounter Bedd Morus on a day of chill mist have an entirely different perception of it. The looming shape seems effortlessly to dominate the narrower, greyer world in which it stands and it is easy to imagine that it was once the focus of long-forgotten beliefs and rituals which were themselves the source of many of the legends and ancient tales handed down to us.

Standing stones such as Bedd Morus are not, however, the last remnants of burial chambers in which the bones and, perhaps, the spirits of a tribe's ancestors were once enshrined. Those tombs had been neglected for many years when the majority of the standing stones were raised, and the society which erected them no longer saw the need to centre their beliefs on the darkened chambers and whispering passage-ways of the old cromlechs.

So, over a span of a thousand years or more, the stones arose, sometimes in pairs, occasionally in groups of three and, in rare cases, in rows of six or more, striding like fossilised giants across the landscape. They supported no other stones, were not part of a larger structure, yet they became, as we shall see, the focal points of well organised and carefully developed ceremonial sites.

Standing stones, or maenhirs, can be found in many parts of the British Isles and beyond. Some, like the stone rows of Carnac in Brittany, are world-famous. Others, such as the Devil's Arrows at Boroughbridge in Yorkshire, or the three Ballachroy stones on the Kintyre Peninsula in Scotland, are known only to archaeologists and students of megal-

The Bedd Morus stone, on Newport Mountain.

ithic astronomy. Many more are celebrated only in their own locality or vanished so long ago that even their exact site is a matter of dispute.

Here in West Wales we are lucky, for many standing stones remain; they lie tumbled in long grasses or rear gauntly in fields of wheat, whilst others dominate stretches of moorland and stand sentinel beside ancient trackways. There are some, smaller and less assertive, which are embedded in hedgerows where harsh banks of nettles cover them.

Yet, however humble and remotely placed these stones may be, we should respect and value them, for they are as much a part of our heritage as the cathedrals and castles which came to dominate the landscape in later times.

The stones, like the buildings, were a visible sign of deeply-held beliefs which shaped people's thoughts and way of life for centuries. They, too, were a focal point, a channel through which people sought to contact and influence the unknown forces which ruled their lives, and whilst all else has vanished, the stones remain; they are, in a sense, the petrified voices of our ancestors.

The purpose of this booklet is therefore to examine the stones, to seek possible reasons for their erection and to recount some of the legends which have come to surround them.

1   BEFORE THE STONES

It is worth noting from the outset that nothing about standing stones is certain and that none of the theories concerning them has been proven beyond doubt. We do not know, and may never know, exactly who built them, when, or why. As the raising and use of these stones were spread over thousands of years it is probable that not all of them were erected for the same purpose. However, as more *is* discovered about them, some of the theories gather weight whilst others are discarded.

The majority of standing stones were believed to have been erected during the early Bronze age, between 3,000 and 4,000 years ago, or even before then. The traditional view was that their appearance followed the arrival in Britain of the famous Beaker People.

These immigrants, or invaders, may have entered the British Isles towards the end of the Neolithic Age at about 2,500 B.C. They were named because of the distinctive incised pottery which they were believed to have introduced and which is found in many sites dating to the period.

The impact of these invaders was once held by archaeologists to have been considerable. Not only were they said to have introduced new styles of pottery, but most important, they also brought with them the craft of metalworking. Their ability to make weapons and other objects in copper, and later bronze, would have given them supremacy over the original native inhabitants; even if they did not conquer the Neolithic peoples completely, they certainly allied themselves with the leaders of the tribes, who were glad of their skills and used them to maintain their own authority.

It is also suggested that in order to find the raw materials for metal working, trade routes were opened up through northern and western Britain.[1] In particular these routes extended to Ireland; one passed through Pembrokeshire via the Presely Hills and out to Whitesands Bay. Part of this trackway still exists along the ridge of the Presely Hills and is called the Golden Road or Via Flamanda (Flemings' Way).

At about this time also, there was an apparent change in burial customs, again attributable to the Beaker People. The interment of the dead in great communal tombs was abandoned and was replaced by individual burials, with grave goods such as pots, weapons or personal ornaments being placed around the body of the dead person. Sometimes, small mounds called round barrows were raised above the graves.

In the years that followed the supposed invasion of the Beaker People the building of stone circles became more frequent, together with the erection of individual standing stones all over the British Isles.

Now, however, this traditional view is being challenged. Some archaeologists believe that the impact of the Beaker people was considerably less than was first thought, and that the changes which took place in Britain at that time were already in motion and were only accelerated by the arrival of the newcomers.

Other archaeologists question the very existence of the Beaker Folk; they put forward the view that the momentous changes which affected Britain at that time were really part of a long, evolving tradition stretching back to the early Neolithic period.[2]

They point out that an improvement in dating methods has shown that many of the 'newer' types of monuments were in fact built earlier than was at first thought. Even the introduction of new pottery, burial customs and metal-working is more likely to have come about as a result of trade and the spread of new ideas, than as a consequence of invasion.[3] It is also possible that the pace of developments was given added impetus by a crisis which seems to have overtaken Britain in the centuries around 3,000 BC.

It would be timely, therefore, to look at the evolving society of the period, at its possible religious beliefs, and at the crisis which befell it.

The Brynmaen stone is one of the tallest in Dyfed.

NOTES

[1] Aubrey Burl, *Rites of the Gods*, p. 131.
[2] Catherine Hills, *Blood of the British*, p. 72.
[3] Ronald Hutton, *The Pagan Religions of the Ancient British Isles*, p. 88.

2 TOMBS AND ANCESTOR HOUSES

Four thousand years ago, the landscape of Britain, though unimaginably wilder than it is today, was far from empty or uncultivated. For many centuries the inhabitants had been clearing forests and wastelands to grow crops, and settlements were already clustered along river banks, beside lakes and on uplands and fertile tracts where cultivation was easiest.

The vast majority of these communities were probably quite small, collections of half-a-dozen or so huts huddled together with fields and grazing grounds surrounding them. The houses were usually round or rectangular in shape, with stone foundations or wooden posts forming the walls. Wattle and daub were no doubt also used, with the whole building capped by a thickly thatched roof.

Several generations of the same family might well occupy a hut. The interior was probably crowded with hunting gear, tools, cooking utensils and personal property; in the centre there burned a fire which was never allowed to go out. The smoke from this formed a thick haze beneath the roof and percolated out through the thatch; quite possibly there was no escape hole for it because the inhabitants knew that the smoke kept the thatch warm and dry and in good condition, as well as discouraging insects.

In the fields wheat, barley, millet, beans and a type of wild pea were grown, whilst cattle, sheep and goats grazed nearby. The surrounding forests and uncultivated land would have provided an annual harvest of nuts and berries, whilst the village hunters would have found plenty of wildlife to end up in the cooking pot.

As well as clearing the forests, it seems that the people of this era also knew how to manage woodland. There is evidence that certain types of trees were grown for specific reasons. Hazel, for instance, was coppiced and the supple poles used for a variety of purposes, including woven hurdles which were laid down to form trackways across the marshy Somerset Levels.[1]

It is also likely that coppiced hazelwood was used for fencing to pen up the cattle and sheep. Certainly, land boundaries had existed for centuries. From both County Mayo in Ireland and from Dartmoor there is evidence of stone-walled fields dating from this and earlier times.[2]

Not far from the villages, perhaps towards the edges of the tribal or family lands, stood the great communal burial chambers. It has been suggested that they, too, were boundary markers, their size and dramatic appearance giving a clear warning of the territorial rights and prestige of their builders.[3]

Certainly, the huge mounds, covered with a crust of tightly-packed stones, or grassed over and bounded by a wall, perhaps of white quartz, dominated the landscape. For many centuries the bones of the dead had been brought to these tombs and within the darkened chamber the spirits of the ancestors were believed to dwell. It may even be that these spirits were thought to have power over the living, or at the very least to be a link with the unimaginable forces which held sway.

It is understandable that beliefs such as these were dominant, for few people in the Neolithic Era lived beyond forty; many died in childhood, or from a horrifying variety of diseases, and even their food supply was dependent on factors beyond their control.

This may explain why many of the tombs had their entrances facing the sectors of the sky where the moon or the sun rose and set. Some archaeologists believe that the idea of the cycle of life, death and rebirth was a prominent one in Neolithic times, with the moon being the symbol of darkness, death and sterility, and the sun being the giver of life, warmth and fertility.[4] Certainly, some of the tombs were carefully aligned to the passage of the sun through the sky, so that the interiors were illuminated on important days of the year by shafts of sunlight which shone down the entrance passages to warm the bones lying within.

The two most famous examples of this can be seen at Newgrange in Ireland and Maes Howe in the Orkney Islands, off the northern coast of Scotland. These two huge burial mounds, built of carefully hewn blocks fitted together and covered by vast mounds of earth, have small apertures above their entrances through which, on one day of the year, sunlight shines; this beam traverses the entrance passage and flowers briefly in the burial chamber where it could be seen only by the spirits of the dead.

The time of this visitation of light was, at both Newgrange and Maes Howe, the midwinter solstice, when the nights are at their longest and the earth is locked in the dead grip of winter.

Belief in the influence exerted by the spirits of the dead may also explain why, as time went by, the focus of the burial mounds shifted from the chambers inside to the great open-air forecourts outside them. Here, ceremonies regularly took place during which the bones of the dead were brought out of the mounds and used as part of the festivities. The meaning of this ritual is lost, but the people may have thought that by involving the remains, and therefore the ghosts, of their ancestors in the ceremonies, the fertility of their crops and of the tribe would be ensured.

The forecourts of the tombs may have been decorated with great coloured poles, rather like the totem-poles of the North American Indians. In the vicinity there would also have been a number of wooden or stone platforms, raised well clear of the ground, upon which the bodies of the dead were laid for some time before being interred. It seems that in many areas of Britain the corpses were left out for the flesh to rot.[5] Perhaps this was for the sake of convenience; a complete body would have been difficult to manoeuvre in through the narrow entrance of a tomb, but it has also been suggested that only by allowing all the flesh to rot away, and even by breaking the bones themselves, did Neolithic people believe the spirit to have been freed.[6]

In some instances the bones were sorted and only certain ones—often the skull and the larger remains—were taken into the tomb.[7] What significance this selection had is uncertain, but it seems likely in any case that only prominent people were buried in such a way.

In some areas, notably in Ireland and in the north and west of Britain, including Wales, these mounds continued to be built and used for some time. Elsewhere, new burial customs were developing; as the long barrows fell into disuse, round barrows were replacing them.

At first, these circular burial places contained large numbers of skeletons, but more frequently they came to contain individual burials. Deep within the cup-shaped mound, a man or woman would be laid with their possessions, the symbols of their prestige, beside them—arrowheads, beads, knives, boars' tusks, and so on. There is also evidence that the dead person was sometimes accompanied into the afterlife by others who were killed for that purpose. Some archaeologists believe that this growing emphasis on individual burial, with grave goods and possibly servants, indicates the rise of a warrior or class elite ruling over large and well organised groups of people.[8]

Other new and different monuments were being built at this time, the uses and functions of which are still not fully understood.

The most enigmatic of all these constructions must be the cursus. This is the name which has been given to a long, narrow enclosure bordered by high banks and ditches. Almost fifty are known in Britain, though they do not occur in every part of the country; there are none in Wales, and most examples occur in Wessex, the Thames Valley, East Anglia, the east and west Midlands, Yorkshire and Scotland.

No one has been able to discover the purpose of these enclosures and archaeological evidence is sparse. They may have developed from the long, banked-up burial chambers and so were connected with rituals of death and burial. A further theory is that they were race-tracks, where tribes competed against one another.

Whatever the truth, one cannot help being impressed by the sheer size of them. The largest, in Dorset, traverses the countryside for more than six miles. Another, on Salisbury Plain, is nearly two miles long.

Another type of monument, predating the cursus but still requiring considerable organisation to build, was the causewayed camp. This consisted of a circular enclosure with surrounding rings of banks and ditches. The entrances to these enclosures lay across causeways over the ditches and through the banks, hence the name given to the structures.

The Mynydd March stone.

Again, it is not clear what purpose these camps served. They may have been places of seasonal assembly,[9] but whether these gatherings were for religious rites or for trade or the settlement of quarrels may never be known.

The causewayed camps, or more likely the crescent-shaped forecourts of the old tombs, may have been the inspiration for another type of monument, known as henges. At first, these circular structures consisted of a bank and ditch, with the ditch placed *inside* the bank as if emphasising that this was a sacred area. Sometimes the henges contained settings of wooden posts; others held rings of stones which in the course of time seem to have replaced the bank and ditch as the most important feature.

Whatever their lineage, these stone circles became a notable feature of life in the late Neolithic and early Bronze Ages, especially in Britain. More than 950 are known in the British Isles, where they are concentrated mostly in the north and west, whilst few are found in Europe.

The circles, which include the most famous prehistoric monuments, Stonehenge and Avebury, were built over a period of some 2,000 years. Some, like Avebury, were enormous and must have been built by a well-organised and hard-working society; others, like Gors Fawr near Mynachlogddu in Pembrokeshire, or the now-destroyed Naw Carreg circle, near Hendre, Carmarthenshire, were small and could have been erected by small family groups.

Even the use of the word 'circle' to describe these monuments is incorrect, for few of them are truly circular in shape; most are egg-shaped or elliptical. Some had a single stone in the middle, whilst others had stones called outliers at some distance from them. There were also those which contained pits full of burnt human bone; whether these were normal burials within an area regarded as sacred, or whether they were placed there so that the spirits of the dead could sanctify and guard the circles, or for both reasons, no one is quite sure. What does seem to be more obvious is that these monuments were linked, like previous ones, to the sun, the moon and the stars.

Many people today are convinced that these circles were built originally for astron-omical purposes. They believe that Neolithic tribes were avid watchers of the skies and used the circles—and individual standing stones—to plot the exact movements of the planetary bodies, even to predict eclipses and other celestial phenomena.

Prehistoric peoples were certainly aware of the movements of the sun and the moon, or they would not have aligned their burial mounds as they did. They were probably able to predict to some extent the solar cycle; primitive societies across the world in recent times have known how to draw up simple astronomical calendars for farming purposes.

But how accurate were these megalithic 'observatories'? It is almost impossible to say; very few seem to have been as perfectly aligned as Maes Howe or Newgrange to the movements of the sun, or are as well preser-ved. Many circles today contain stones which have toppled over, or have been removed, entirely destroying any alignments which may have existed. Even the shape of the sky-line itself may have been altered by human action over the centuries, whilst in other places the ground level has changed. The Royal Commission for Ancient Monuments, in its inventory for Carmarthenshire published in the 1920s, recorded two separate sites where local people could remember that, in their own lifetime, the ground around standing stones had become boggy, so that the stones had sunk and tilted by several feet. A number of other maenhirs were reported to have been taken from their original sites in fairly recent times and were re-erected elsewhere.

If the same picture of loss, change and interference is true for the rest of Britain, then the difficulties encountered by experts attempting to interpret these sites can be readily appreciated.

However, most archaeologists would agree that stone circles do seem to have been erected with some sort of astronomic purpose in mind and that they were used for rituals and celebrations.

Quite a number of sites have folk-tales associating them with dancing, or with games during which the participants are turned into stone for breaking the Sabbath. Perhaps these are indeed folk memories of what once went on within the rings. What-ever form these celebrations took, they could

The Waun Mawn stone.

One of the outlying stones at Gors Fawr Circle.

The Tafarn y Bwlch stones.

The Sythfaen stone.

St. Paul's Marble.

have been a development of the rituals which had taken place long before in the forecourts of the old tombs.

One thing is worth mentioning; in the centuries following the appearance of the first small circles, Neolithic Britain seems to have undergone some great changes. From about 3,300 B.C. onwards, for a period of some four or five hundred years, the building of large monuments appears to have ceased. Those which had been constructed and had been in use for some time gradually became neglected. The megalithic tombs were deliberately closed off, in some cases filled with stones or other rubble. The number of round barrows being built increased, as if there had been a major change in religious ideas.

In many areas, fields were no longer cultivated and became overgrown; from Wessex and East Anglia comes evidence that land which had for centuries been cultivated, was neglected and became choked with weeds. In other parts of Britain there was a regeneration of scrubland and forest which had formerly been cleared. Some upland areas were abandoned by their populations, which moved down into the adjacent lowlands.

It is unlikely that a change of climate produced these differences. It is more likely that, because the land had been exploited for generations to provide food-stuffs for growing numbers of people, the soil eventually became exhausted and there was a collapse of the agricultural system, with a resulting

18

shortage of food.[10] There may even have been a series of famines, spread over many years.

If all this did happen, then the shock to the social order must have been severe; a period of instability, even chaos, can be imagined. Life for the inhabitants of Britain became even harder and many people must have felt that their gods had turned against them.

Gradually, however, new power structures arose and by about 2,500 B.C., the building of the great circular monuments was resumed on a larger scale than before; Stonehenge and Avebury as we know them date from this period.

It is against this background of a long-evolving tradition of religious belief, at a time of change and uncertainty, that the majority of standing stones were erected. Their purpose and use may have varied over the centuries, and from area to area, but the basic underlying thoughts of the builders must have been the same; the stones, like the tombs and the circles, were linked with death, burial, the sun and moon and rebirth.

NOTES

[1] Oliver Rackham, *The History of the Countryside*, p. 382.

[2] Catherine Hills, *Blood of the British*, p. 36, 37.

[3] Catherine Hills, *Blood of the British*, p. 50.

[4] Aubrey Burl, *Rites of the Gods*, p. 67.

[5] Euan Mackie, *The Megalith Builders*, p. 76, 79. Aubrey Burl, *Rites of the Gods*, p. 73.

[6] Aubrey Burl, *Rites of the Gods*, p. 72.

[7] Catherine Hills, *The Blood of the British*, p. 52. Aubrey Burl, *Rites of the Gods*, p. 74.

[8] S. Pierpont, *Social Patterns:—Yorkshire Prehistory*, p. 212-242. R. Hutton, *The Pagan Religions of the Ancient British Isles*, p. 68.

[9] R. Hutton, *The Pagan Religions of the Ancient British Isles*, p. 49.

[10] R. Hutton, *The Pagan Religions of the Ancient British Isles*, p. 51. Geoffrey Wainwright, *The Henge Monuments*, p. 29-30.

3 THE RAISING OF THE STONES

West Wales is particularly rich in standing stones; between seventy and one hundred remain in Pembrokeshire, with similar numbers for Carmarthenshire and Cardiganshire. Many of these are shown on Ordnance Survey maps, particularly the 1:25,000 scale, but there are others which do not appear. This is, perhaps, because their provenance is uncertain; they may be cattle-rubbing stones, many of which were erected in the eighteenth and nineteenth centuries; they may have fallen and as a result are difficult to find; others are omitted because they have been dragged from their original sites for use as gate-posts or were broken up for building materials.

The fact that removal often involved the use of teams of men and horses, even dynamite, only makes all the more remarkable the sheer hard work originally necessary to raise them.

Most of the stones in West Wales were probably erected, as already mentioned, by quite small groups of people. It seems likely that they were taken from the nearest convenient source, even though in many cases this must have involved dragging them for a considerable distance. Sandstone was quite frequently used, whilst other maenhirs are of quartz, grey gritstone or ingenous rock. Few consist of Presely bluestone, despite the theory that the bluestone source, Carn Meini, and the surrounding area was a site so sacred that Bronze Age people transported stones from there to erect them at Stonehenge.

It is quite possible that many of the stones had already been detached from the parent rock by the natural action of wind, rain and frost; it is also equally likely that other stones were deliberately detached. One method of doing this would be by a slow, laborious chipping away at a natural fault in the rock face. Another way might have been through the use of fire to split the rock, though this might also open up other, hidden fissures within it.

There must also have been a number of boulders littering the countryside, left-overs from the glacial movements of the Ice Age and these could have been appropriated fairly easily for use.

These pillars of rock were chosen for their shape; a surprising number are irregularly shaped triangles, squares or rectangles with two or three relatively broad sides, the remaining faces being thin. An extreme example of this can be found near St. Ishmael's in Pembrokeshire; the Mabe's Gate Stone is a slab of laminated sandstone about 10ft high with its 'front and back' faces measuring 7ft across, but with a thickness of less than one foot.

The height of these stones varies a good deal. Some are small, no more than three or four feet tall, whilst others tower up to ten or even fourteen feet in height. The variation in size may reflect the use to which the stones were put, or merely the numbers of people erecting and using them.

Some of the maenhirs seem to have been deliberately shaped, for many taper to a point or at least are narrower at the top. In other parts of Britain, particularly in the north and in Ireland, stones were decorated with carvings. This was presumably done before they were erected. The carvings usually consist of a ring-and-cup marks (a hollow in the surface surrounded by a ring), though sometimes the rings and cups are separated from one another. Shapes resembling axe-heads were also featured, as well as spirals, semi-circles and even foot shapes. The exact meaning of these various symbols and designs is, however, uncertain.

Few examples have been found in Wales, and most of those that do exist are in the north. The Trellyfaint stone, near Nevern in Pembrokeshire, has ring-and-cup marks, though it is actually the capstone of a burial chamber.

Another Pembrokeshire maenhir which may have been decorated can be found at Sampson's Cross, near Bosherston, several miles south of Pembroke. This large stone, made of igneous rock, has on its south-

The Mabe's Gate Maenhir.

eastern face two circular hollows which do not seem to be natural flaws in the rock.

One of the pillars, now fallen, in the row of stones known as Parc y Meirw (the Field of the Dead), near Fishguard, may have been carved,[2] though its companion stones were not.

The stone known as Maen Llwyd was incised with what appeared to be the outline of a bow and arrow. This unusual carving is probably an unfinished cross within a circle; many stones were carved with crosses by early churchmen who sought to 'Christian-ise', or even to destroy entirely, the old pagan relics.

The question of how the stones were moved from their source to the place where they were raised has exercised the imagination of a great number of people. It has been suggested that the stones were pulled vertically upright, or placed horizontally on the ground, then 'walked' along rather as a heavy wardrobe is moved across a room, first one corner and then the next being pushed forward. Although this is a possibility, the dangers of the method are only too apparent; a vertical stone could easily topple over and crush the pulling team. If the stone was horizontal then it would require a tremendous effort to move it, especially over rough ground.

Archaeologists favour the idea of wooden rollers, or even strong wooden sledges, with teams of men pulling at the front, whilst others at the back held guide ropes to prevent the sledge from veering from side to side or from careering past the pullers on a slope.[3] Long trusses of grass would have been laid down to ease the passage of the sledge, with any small hollows in the ground being filled in first.

The sites for the placing of the stones were carefully prepared; even today the remains of platforms built into sloping ground are visible at a number of sites.

At Pen-bont Rhydybeddau to the east of Aberystwyth for example, two stones known as Cerrig yr Ŵyn (the stones of the lamb), stand in a large field overlooking the valley. The field slopes westwards in a series of terraces and the ground around each stone appears to have been carefully levelled off into a rough platform. The setting, with the valley floor opening out to the north and west, is truly spectacular!

The surface area at every site was no doubt cleared of small boulders and pebbles and then the socket hole was dug to receive the stone. This pit was carefully shaped; if it was too small the stone would not have fitted and if too big the pillar would have toppled over. Possibly a ramp was dug on one side leading down into the hole, with the earth piled up on the opposite lip to act as a support.

The raising of a large stone would have been a hair-raising business, especially if the work teams were inexperienced or few in

The Maenhir at Sampson's Cross may bear traces
of Bronze Age carving.

Maen Llwyd, carved with an unfinished cross.

number. The only resource which was available to them was man-power, with ropes to pull on and stong wooden poles for support.

Once the stone had been manoeuvred down the ramp with its base fitting into the socket hole, it would have been pulled into an upright position and held there using the ropes and wooden supports whilst smaller stones, earth and clay were quickly packed in around the base. Only when all these had been tightly rammed down, and everyone was satisfied that the stone would not fall, would the support be removed.

There is evidence that, before the raising of some maenhirs, the cremated remains of bodies were placed in the socket holes.[4] It is therefore likely that the raising of a stone was accompanied by ritual celebrations, though we shall probably never know exactly what form they took.

It has also been suggested that stones were sometimes painted or stained with natural dyes, perhaps to emphasise their sacred and ceremonial nature. Even in our own century there were maenhirs in Ireland and Scotland which were annually whitewashed. (There is a stone in Pembrokeshire which is still decorated in this way, though no one knows if this is an ancient or a relatively modern tradition, or why it began.)

It would be interesting to know what were the criteria by which Bronze Age peoples chose the sites for their stones. Was it because an area already contained other, older, monuments and was regarded as sacred? Some stones were certainly erected close to earlier monuments, though an equal number appear not to have been. Perhaps the stones imparted their own sanctity to a hitherto non-sacred site, which would explain why some maenhirs are associated with monuments of a contemporary or later date.

It is difficult, some 4,000 years later, to picture the surroundings in which these stones originally stood. We cannot be sure if they stood in forest clearings or in the midst of cultivated areas, or of their proximity to settlements. Their sacred nature may have meant that they were erected well away from any habitation.

Few stones seem to have been placed on the summits of hills or ridges, where they would have been visible for great distances; many are to be found on valley sides, or on sloping ground. Others are situated on relatively flat stretches, with a semi-circle of hills or rising ground to provide a back-drop.

Water also seems to have been an important factor in the siting of the maenhirs. A glance at an Ordnance Survey map will show that many of them are within easy reach of streams and rivers; the long axes of the stones often point towards the water courses.[5] Water was obviously vital to those early communities, but did it, as a life-giving force, also play an important role in their ritual beliefs?

As well as being raised singly, stones were also erected in pairs, or even in settings of three or more. Some of the pairs still remain; the two known as Cerrig Meibion Arthur, near Mynachlogddu in Pembrokeshire, have attracted a rich folklore, though the pair situated on either side of the narrow lane separating the farms of Hendy and Gilfaen at Llangain, south-west of Carmarthen, are less well-known.

Pairs of stones often have similar features. One of the stones may be taller with a squarish top, whilst the second will be smaller and will taper to a point; the Buwch a'r Llo (cow and calf) stones, to the east of Aberystwyth, are a good example of this. Other pairs may consist of a triangular stone set near a rectangular one, or a wide boulder next to a slender one.[6] The combinations are various, though in Pembrokeshire, at least, the tall, square shape against the small pointed one seems most frequent.[7]

Some people believe that pillars such as these are meant to represent the male and female idea and that this indicates that the maenhirs were once the focus of a fertility cult.[8]

There was also a link with death and the after life. Excavations have often revealed that burial pits lie between the stones, or close by.

Alignments of three or more stones are comparatively rare. The most famous example in Wales is the group called the Harold Stones at Trelleck in Monmouthshire. There are few surviving examples in West Wales, though the two stones near Tremaenhir Farm, near Solva, are said to be all that is left of a threesome. Another setting of three stones existed near

Cerrig Meibion Arthur, the subjects of a rich and
ancient folklore.

The Buwch a'r Llo stones are typical of the many
pairs of stones to be found in Dyfed.

Parc y Meirw one of the most famous alignments
of stones in Wales.

Dolgwm House in the parish of Llanllawddog; only two remain upright, the third having fallen.

At Llech Ciste, in Carmarthenshire, there exists a setting of four stones; two small pillars flank a 10 ft megalith and a fourth stone stands nearby.

One alignment, a row of eighteen stones, none more than 3 ft high, can be found on Mynydd Llanybydder, near Llanybydder; it is not marked on Ordnance Survey maps. The Royal Commission for Ancient Monuments, in its 1925 volume on Carmarthenshire, noted that during the latter half of the 19th century, the stones had sunk by a considerable amount into the surrounding ground. The site is now lost in a thick plantation of conifers.

One of the most famous alignments of stones in West Wales is the row known as Parc y Meirw (the field of the Dead), near Llanllawern in Pembrokeshire. Here, eight large stones stretched for 40 metres or more along a deep lane leading down a gently sloping hillside. Only four of the stones remain upright today, in the hedge bordering the lane, but even so the row and its setting, overlooking Fishguard Harbour, is impressive.

It is easy, in such panoramic surroundings, to appreciate why many people believe that pillars such as these were once used to study the movements of the stars—but do these and other theories contain any truth?

NOTES

[1] J.M. Lewis, 'The Standing Stones of Pembrokeshire': *Pembrokeshire Historian No. 2*, p. 9.

[2] *Archaeologia Cambrensis*, 1868, p. 178.

[3] R.J.C. Atkinson, *Stonehenge: Archaeology and Interpretation*, p. 105-116.

[4] Aubrey Burl, *Rites of the Gods*, p. 197-201.

[5] *Archaeologia Cambrensis*, 1989, p. 21.

[6] Aubrey Burl *From Carnac to Callanish* p. 181.

[7] J.M. Lewis 'The Standing Stones of Pembrokeshire' *Pembrokeshire Historian No. 2* p. 10.

[8] Aubrey Burl *Rites of the Gods* p. 197-201.

4   THE PURPOSE OF THE STONES

In 1875, E.L. Barnwell, writing in *Archaeologia Cambrensis*, made the following statement: '(the) evidence that the maenhir is or was nothing more than a tombstone or funeral monument is so extensive or so conclusive that it is unnecessary to discuss the question. The process by which it has changed its character in the course of time is a simple and natural one. The reverence originally shown the defunct chief or warrior is easily transferred to his monument which in time becomes an object of religious worship. When this has passed away in its turn the monument still remains as an invaluable landmark.'

At first glance, Barnwell's ideas seem to be supported by a body of evidence. There are many instances from all over Britain of stones which are said to mark the resting place of famous—or infamous—people; the Bedd Morus stone, for example, is said to have been erected over the grave of an outlaw.

There are also stones which stand close to or on the perimeters of burial mounds, as at the recently excavated sites at Parc Maen near Llangolman, Pembrokeshire, and Aber Camddwr in the upper Rheidol Valley of Cardiganshire. (see Chapter 5). There are also maenhirs which are now free-standing but which originally were entirely enclosed within a barrow; over the centuries, the mound has been worn away or ploughed out, leaving the stone visible. Indeed, there are probably some unexcavated burial mounds which still hide, at their core, a stone pillar. A classic example of this was the unexpected discovery by Sir Cyril Fox of a small standing stone within the barrow he was excavating on Kilpaison Burrows, Rhoscrowther, in the early 1920s. [1]

We do not know the purpose of these buried stones, though it has been suggested that they may have been intended as guardian stones, embodying the spirits of the dead. [2]

Excavation of maenhir sites had also revealed the presence of small pits containing nothing more than a layer of charcoal, but others have held the cremated remains of human bones. Fragments of human bone have also been discovered set into the socket holes of the maenhirs themselves. These burials are not likely to have been of important people, with the stones as markers; it is more probably that they were dedicatory, placed carefully into the prepared hole immediately before the raising of the stone, their presence hallowing it in some way, possibly imparting to it and the surrounding area an extra sanctity and power.

If archaeologists are correct in assuming that death and fertility were linked in the minds of Bronze Age peoples, then it is easy to understand why these stones may also have been the focus of a fertility cult, as many modern writers believe they were. These writers claim that the rich tradition of folk-lore and legend which surrounds many standing stones is in fact a folk memory of the type of rituals and beliefs which were centred on the sites during the Bronze Age. A surprising number of these old tales have elements in common; dancing, water, the devil, the punishment of Sabbath law-breakers, and the power of the stones to heal or make fertile.

One of the most famous examples of this type of folk-lore in Britain is that of the Roll-right stones in Oxfordshire. The pillars of this circle are said to go to drink at a spring on New Year's Eve and chippings taken from the stones were said to ward off illness. Similarly, the Tippet stones on Bodmin Moor and the Merry Maidens near Land's End in Cornwall are supposed to be the remains of dancers, petrified as a punishment for dancing on the Sabbath.

In West Wales, the best known dancing stones are the three pillars to be found in the vicinity of Bosherston, south of Pembroke. Two stones named the Devil's Quoit and one named the Harold Stone are said to leave their places once a year and to meet at a ford to drink and dance. The devil sits upon one of the stones playing a flute, whilst a coven of witches whirls round in a frenzied dance.

These legends may of course date back to the time when Christianity was establishing

The Harold Stone, Stackpole, one of the three
'dancing stones' of Pembrokeshire.

itself in the British Isles. The church was anxious then, and during later centuries, to wipe out all traces of earlier religions, and often destroyed or took over the ancient sacred sites. The old tombs and standing stones were deliberately linked with tales of devils, goblins and the punishment of evil-doers as a warning to the newly converted and as a way of denigrating ancient beliefs.

This campaign was frequently unsuccess-ful, which says much for the power that the stones have continued to exercise over the minds of people down to our present century. In many areas of Britain, Ireland and Brittany there are traditions which specifically link the stones with human fertility.

The Rollright Stones, for example, were visited, up to the 18th century at least, by childless women who believed that to increase their chances of pregnancy they had to touch the Kingstone with their bare breasts. The maenhir of Plouarzel in Brittany was similarly resorted to by newly married couples. The pillar bore round bosses on two of its faces, about three feet from the ground; the man would rub his chest against one of these projections, whilst the woman would rub herself on the other. In this way, the man would ensure that he became the father of sons, whilst the woman would become the ruler of the man and his house.

None of the stones in West Wales is reputed nowadays to have these attributes, but an echo of the old beliefs may be found in the traditions surrounding the Love Stone. This maenhir now lies in the yard of Loveston Farm, near Pembroke, and in past centuries courting couples came to it and promised before witnesses to marry and be faithful to one another.

A belief in the healing power of stones has also persisted through the centuries, and was particularly strong during the medieval period. At Canna's Well in Llangan West parish, in Pembrokeshire, the sick offered a pin at the well and then bathed in the water and drank it. Following this they would then lie down to sleep on Canna's Chair, a megalith situated a few yards from the well. If the treatment failed in the first instance, it would be repeated for up to 14 days. These pilgrimages continued until the 1830s when much of the soil between the well and the

water-course was carried away and the water supply dried up. [3]

Sometimes the megaliths could heal minor ailments as well as more serious ones. It was believed, for instance, that rainwater taken from a crack in the top of a stone which stands in the garden of Dolgwm House, six miles to the north-east of Carmarthen, was an excel-lent cure for warts. [4] This stone is one of three, all situated close to one another, which are known as Meini Gwyn, the white stones; 'white' maenhirs, made from quartz or lime-stone or other pale coloured rock, were believed to possess especially powerful healing qualities.

It is possible that Bronze Age peoples believed that the life-giving powers of the stones were derived from the sun. There is evidence that the earth itself had from the earliest times been worshipped as a Mother Goddess and it is not unlikely that the stones were the channel through which, at the onset of Spring, the barren soil was made fertile.

Many people today believe that individual stones were used to study the movements of the sun and moon, or of the stars. It has been suggested that this was done for agricultural purposes; or because the star-watchers were anxious to know when these celestial bodies were at their most powerful; or because the planets, by their various ascendancies and settings, marked the times of the year when the spirits of the dead were at their most powerful and could be more easily contacted by the living; or for a combination of all these reasons.

This may or may not be true. If, as some archaeologists think, stone circles were aligned to the movements of the sun, moon and stars, then there is no reason why indiv-idual maenhirs could not also have served the same purpose. The night skies at that time were presumably clearer than they are today, when the stars are often dimmed by the glow of street lights and the haze caused by indust-rialisation. It would have been relatively easy for people in the Bronze Age to monitor the movements of the sun or of a particular star and so notice the points along the horizon at which it rose or set.

Aubrey Burl, amongst others, believes that these alignments would have been built up slowly, over many years of study. He suggests that, whichever planetary body was under

One of the three white stones known collectively
as Meini Gwyn.

observation, the points at which it rose or set along the horizon, or the point of its highest ascendancy, could have been marked with a wooden stake. Thus, a whole arc of stakes might develop, until eventually the wooden markers were replaced by more permanent stone ones; from such beginnings, the idea of building whole circles of stone may have developed.

In the same way, single standing stones, or rows of them, may have been preceded by wooden posts. There is evidence from a number of sites that the socket holes for stones were dug into earlier post holes and that the stones were frequently surrounded by a complex arrangement of wooden posts or stakes.

The possible link between stars and standing stones has proved to be such a fascinating one, that during the last hundred years or so, many enthusiasts have tried to work out possible alignments for pillars in West Wales.

The Reverend W. Done Bushell, writing in *Archaeologia Cambrensis* in 1911, suggested that the Budloy Stone, near Maenclochog in Pembrokeshire, was aligned with Alcyone, the brightest star of the Pleiades cluster. He believed that at Beltane, the Celtic Mayday Festival, Alcyone rose about one hour and forty minutes before the sun and might therefore have been regarded as the herald of the dawn.

The Rev. Bushell also pointed out that the stones of the circle at Gors Fawr would have been aligned to the rising of Arcturus, whilst Professor Alexander Thom believed that the two maenhirs standing outside the circle were aligned to the midsummer sunrise over the summit of Foel Drych. Furthermore, Professor Thom put forward the idea that the stone row at Parc y Meirw was in a direct line with the moon at its minimum, or most south-westerly, settings.

The point lay to the west-north-west, but another focus could have lain up the sloping hillside to the east-south-east. A megalithic tomb known as 'Arthur's Quoit' once stood in this direction, but it was destroyed in 1844 and the rubble was used to build a house. Perhaps it is no coincidence that the land rises to the east south-east, and that the stones of the row increase in height towards the tallest there, a huge stone some 11 feet tall.[5]

We may never know the truth about these alignments, but the possibility that they exist and that circles and individual stones were used as astronomic observatories will be hotly debated for many years to come!

There is also the theory that the stones were intended as waymarkers; there are many which stand beside ancient track-ways or even modern roads. Bedd Morus and the stone known as Y Garreg Hir, overlooking the Gwaun valley, are obvious examples, whilst on Mynydd Malláen, north of Llandovery, the Malláen stone guards what may be an extremely old way over the mountains. To the east of Aberystwyth, between Penbont Rhydybeddau and Ponterwyd, six stones

Y Garreg Hir, Pembrokeshire, stands beside an ancient trackway.

are spread along or near several long-established, inter-connected roads.

Few of these pillars are, however, visible from great distances away, and they must have been less conspicuous in the Bronze Age when forest covered much more of the land than it does today. It is also difficult to understand, even in areas of open landscape, how isolated maenhirs would have been of much use to travellers unless the routes were then more regularly punctuated by stones than they are today. The maenhirs could, however, have marked out those sections which were indeterminate, or where two or more routes met.

There is also another possible explanation. The routes could have been developed in order to link up, and provide access to, sites which were already sacred. These places, whether they contained old barrows, newly raised stones or a combination of both, would have been regularly visited, and a network of paths would have quickly sprung into existence. Alternatively, perhaps some of the sites were deliberately placed near established trade routes for ease of access.

Some maenhirs were no doubt placed close to the edge of tribal or family territories, just as the old long barrows were, in order to establish a claim to the area. The use of the stones as boundary markers may have lingered on for thousands of years, for there are many stones in Britain which, even today, stand on or near old county, manorial or parish boundaries.

The stone known as Hirfaen Gwyddog is a good example of this. Over 15 feet high, it stands some three miles south-east of Lampeter on the boundary between the old counties of Carmarthenshire and Cardiganshire. It is first mentioned in an entry written upon the margin of one of the pages of the eighth century Gospel of St. Chad. The entry refers to a gift of land to the Church of Llandaff, one of the boundaries being 'behet hirmaen guidauc'—'as far as hirfaen gwyddog'. In using as a territorial boundary a stone which was obviously already a famous landmark, the medieval chronicles may well have been following a long-established local tradition. It is worth noting that in subsequent centuries the stone was used again for the same purpose; the later history is detailed in Chapter 7.

There is no doubt that, in the Bronze Age, large groups of people would gather at these stones and that the pillars continued to be used as places of assembly for many centuries. A huge maenhir known as Yr Eisteddfa once stood near Ffynnon y Groes (Well of the Cross), in Cardiganshire. Its name suggests that, in addition to marking a well site, it was also used as a meeting place; it was, alas, broken up for building materials in the 1840s. A similar fate awaited a stone in Loveston parish, several miles north east of Pembroke; up until the early years of the nineteenth century it had always been used as the location for sports and festivals.

A number of stones in West Wales are associated with battles. There are three stones in Pembrokeshire, one near Bosherton, another near Broad Haven and the third on Skomer Island, which are said to mark the sites of victories by King Harold II over Viking invaders.[6] All three are called the Harold Stone because of this; however, the stones all date from the Bronze Age and Harold's supposed battles must have taken place in the years before 1066, when he was killed at Hastings. As there is no evidence that the king visited Pembrokeshire, these tales must be examples of much later legends attaching themselves to already existing monuments. Perhaps recollections of Harold's victory over the Danes at Stamford Bridge became confused with folk-memories of fighting in the vicinity of the stones.

Other maenhirs also have their battle legends; a desperate struggle between two armies is said to have taken place around the pillars of Parc y Meirw, but the identity of the combatants is lost.[7] Similarly, Carreg Goch, near Llangyndeyrn is reputed to be the site of a battle, whilst Cerrig Meibion Arthur, in the Presely Hills, is said to mark the spot where some of King Arthur's warriors were killed by the boar Twrch Trwyth.

Of all the theories concerning the stones, the ones concerning battles are the hardest to prove. Although legends may contain a germ of truth, archaeological evidence is lacking.

There is available, however, a large body of evidence, all of it gleaned by archaeologists in recent years, which does answer some of the puzzling questions about standing stones—whilst at the same time posing other equally fascinating and frustrating ones!

John 1993

Y Garreg Goch is reputed to mark the site of a
fierce battle.

The Budloy Maenhir.

The Lady Stone, Dinas.

NOTES

[1] *Archaeologia Cambrensis*, 1926, p. 7.
[2] Aubrey Burl, *Rites of the Gods*, p. 55, 56.
[3] Francis Jones, *The Holy Wells of Wales*, p. 204.
[4] Paul Davies, *Historic West Wales*, p. 38.
[5] Aubrey Burl, *From Carnac to Callanish*, p. 99.
[6] Gerald of Wales, *The Journey through Wales*, and *The Description of Wales*, p. 268. Richard Fenton, *Historical Tour through Pembrokeshire*, p. 88.
[7] *Archaeologia Cambrensis*, 1868, p. 177.

This maenhir on Mynydd Mallaen may mark an ancient trackway.

The Devil's Quoit, one of the 'dancing stones' of Pembrokeshire.

5   THE EXCAVATIONS

During the last three decades, a number of standing stones in West Wales have been excavated; they include sites at Rhos y Clegyrn, Stackpole, St. Ishmaels and Parc Maen in Pembrokeshire, Ffos y Maen in Carmarthenshire and Aber Camddwr in Cardiganshire. Although there were finds at each site which were different, there were also a remarkable number of similarities, which indicate that these particular stones, if not others, were erected with the same purpose in mind. A more detailed description of the excavations is contained in the Appendix, but for the purposes of this chapter the findings are summarised.

One of the first stones to be excavated, in 1962 and in 1965-68, was the Rhos y Clegyrn stone, near St. Nicholas in Pembrokeshire. This pillar of igneous rock, almost nine feet high, stands on a stretch of marshy, gorse-covered land. Close by is a low ringbank some three to four feet high, which was at first believed to be the remains of a round barrow or cairn. Within a radius of a mile from the site stood two other stones, two burial chambers and a round barrow.

The excavation revealed that the ring bank might well have been the setting for a circle of stones; these had all disappeared, presumably dragged away at some date after 1811, when Richard Fenton, the Pembrokeshire antiquarian, described the site as having 'a large druidical circle with one of the encircling stones on the south side supereminent above its fellows, being about eleven feet high above the ground'.[1]

The Pembrokeshire Archaeological Survey, published in 1908, records this circle as measuring 27 yards by 22 yards. There were also traces of an inner circle with a circumference of about 8 yards.

Strangely, Fenton did not mention in his description the maenhir which remains today, possibly because when he visited the area it was dwarfed by the nearby circle and was not the prominent feature it has since become. The modern excavators, however, found much that would have fascinated him.

The excavations at Rhos y Clegyrn provided a wealth of information for archaeologists.

The stone itself was set into a carefully prepared hole some 2ft 6ins deep; this socket had been packed with stones all around except on the eastern side. Here was found a smaller pit filled with clay in which stood two small pillar stones. Beneath the largest of these lay sherds of pottery.

About twenty-four feet to the east of the maenhir were the remains of a second large stone which appeared to have been pulled down in comparatively recent times. Traces of its socket hole were discernable some twelve feet to the north. This hole also appeared to have been carefully dug, but was filled only with humus, together with several broken pieces of stone of the same type as the fallen pillar.

A series of small pits was also uncovered. The perimeters of some of these had been marked with a rim of small stones, whilst others contained stones which had once been upright, but which had subsequently been levelled, the pits being then packed with clay. There were further pits which seemed to have been filled with layers of charcoal or in which upright wooden posts had once stood.

In several places there were also hollow rings of stone between three or four feet in diameter. Some fragments of cremated bone were found about twenty feet from the upright stone, surrounded by a scatter of pot-sherds.

One of the most intriguing, yet inexplicable, features of the site were the settings of stones which appeared to make patterns of straight, concentric or curved lines.

Most of these discoveries lay in the area between the two maenhirs and stretched in a roughly oval shape to the north of them; this area seemed to be given definition by the pits already mentioned and by sections of cobbling. The cobbling had been closely and carefully laid in sections, but did not cover the whole area. Some of the pits lay outside it, as did the fallen stone.

The archaeologists believed that this oval area, which seemingly linked the two maenhirs, was proof that they had originally been intended as a pair and not as separate features of the site.

At Ffos y Maen, the standing stone was found to be surrounded by a cobbled area which had possibly once been boat shaped. At Stackpole something even more surprising was discovered; over 3,000 small stones had been arranged in upright rows to form a trapezoidal shape extending roughly north-eastwards away from the maenhir. The archaeologists who excavated the stone considered that distinct alignments existed within this setting,[2] but were unable at the time to draw any firm conclusions as to what they might be.

It is fascinating to conjecture as to what these cobbled areas might have been. Were they sacred areas around the maenhirs, their tiny stones aligned with natural features along the horizon, where the planets appeared or sank from sight; or were the stones organised into patterns which were thought to have special power and significance?

Here, on festive occasions, the tribes or family groups could have gathered, perhaps on nights of the full moon, or to watch for the first glimpse of sunrise over a distant hill and to take part in rituals of great potency.

There may also have been round houses adjacent to many of these maenhirs. Before the stone known as the Devil's Quoit was erected at Stackpole, a circular timber hut had occupied the site. There were definite traces of such a structure, possibly even two, at St. Ishmael's,[3] whilst at Parc Maen a number of post holes seemed to have been arranged in a circle.

There is no proof from any of these places that the huts formed part of a village. Exactly the opposite seems to have been true. The huts were built in isolation and therefore may have been occupied by the guardians of the site. Alternatively, they may have been ritual in purpose. Perhaps the tribe, or certain members of it, gathered in the flickering gloom beneath the thatched roof for special ceremonies from which all others were barred, so sacred were the rites to be enacted.

Two of the sites, Parc Maen and Aber Camddwr, included burial cairns adjacent to the stones. These mounds had been constructed during the Bronze Age, but in neither case were human remains discovered, possibly because of the surrounding acidic soil. At Aber Camddwr, the cairn had been in existence for several hundred years before the maenhirs were erected, evidence of the continuing use of the area as a sacred place.

At every one of the excavations mentioned in this chapter, numerous small pits were discovered. Some of these holes held fillings of charcoal which occasionally included fragments of bone, whilst others had obviously held wooden posts. In some cases, the post-

This shapely stone at Tremaenhir Farm is one of
three which once stood at this site.

holes had been subsequently enlarged to hold the stones themselves. The number of posts which had been erected varied considerably, from one at Stackpole to over one hundred at Aber Camddwr.

The holes were often widely separated, or gathered in curves or semi-circles. There was sometimes no pattern or arrangement to be discerned.

During the Bronze Age, the posts they held must have been a dominating feature of each site, but their purpose is unclear. Were they part of the tracery of alignments suspected by archaeologists, or were they burial markers; could they have been some sort of cult image, carved and painted as were the totem poles of the North American Indians?

We also do not know exactly what the religious beliefs of Bronze Age peoples were. It is probable that the earth, the moon and, in particular, the sun were worshipped as gods. Many carvings dating to the period, especially the 'cup and ring' marks, have been interpreted as sun or moon symbols.[4] In Scandinavia there are carvings which show warriors bearing aloft what may be a sun symbol. Nor should it be forgotten that many monuments from the Bronze Age, and earlier, seem to be aligned to the south and south-west sectors of the sky, through which the moon and sun travel daily.

The journeys of these planetary bodies were no doubt carefully studied, for they affected the lives of the people. In summer the sun rode high in the sky, its warmth bringing the earth to life, nourishing and ripening the fruits of the soil. Winter, when the sun was low on the horizon, its strength waning, must have been the season most feared; it was a time of coldness and barenness, even of death, from which the earth might never awake if the proper rituals were not observed.

The standing stones were probably the focus of these carefully planned rites. Their importance was frequently emphasised by the placing of dedicatory burials beneath them and perhaps this gave them a doubly vital role; as receptacles for the spirits of the dead and as a channel through which the power of the sun could be drawn down to replenish the earth.

The organisation of this religion was likely to have been in the hands of a priesthood which was either part of the ruling elite, or closely allied to it. The forecasting of astronomical events, the interpretation of omens and portents, the organisation of sacred rituals, were mysteries understood only by members of this group and the knowledge was no doubt used as a means of preserving their own power, as well as a way of communicating with the supernatural.

All this is, of course, pure speculation. We do not know what form these rituals took, and more important, we do not know how the sun, moon, death and fertility were combined in Bronze Age religion. The archaeological evidence in this respect is scarce and experts are rightly wary of drawing hard and fast conclusions from it.

What does seem certain is that towards the end of the Bronze Age, further great changes occurred in Britain and Europe and as a result, many of the great ritual centres fell into disuse.

NOTES

[1] Richard Fenton, *Historical Tour through Pembrokeshire*, p. 15.
[2] *Current Archaeology*, No. 82, p. 339.
[3] *Archaeologia Cambrensis*, 1989.
[4] Ronald Hutton, *The Pagan Religions of the Ancient British Isles*, pp. 104, 108.

6   THE FATE OF THE STONES

After about 1500 B.C., no new large centres were constructed; the society which had built and maintained them for so long seems to have entered into a rapid decline. The reasons for this are uncertain, but there is evidence for a great movement of populations on the Continent.[1] Whether this was due to warfare and invasion, or because good agricultural land was becoming scarce, is uncertain. Some archaeologists think that over-intensive farming had destroyed the root systems which held together the soil so that some upland areas were denuded, whilst other sections of arable land were exhausted.[2]

If this did happen, then whole tribes could well have set out to search for new, fresh land on which to live, displacing other settled societies as they went. As the centres of population shifted, so would the old trade routes, causing further disruption. It is also likely that at about this time the climate altered, becoming cooler and wetter and adding to the agricultural problems.[3]

As society changed, so did its beliefs and religion change and develop. There were many new gods now to worship, though these may well have had their origins in the older deities and spirits worshipped around the standing stones and ancient tombs.

From about 1,000 B.C., onwards, during the years which saw the development of the Iron Age, many of the long barrows and ancient henges were destroyed, especially where settlements were most thickly clustered.[4]

The old sites were, however, still powerful and their influence lingered on. With the coming of Christianity to Britain, this was seen as a challenge; the early missionaries established themselves wherever possible in the old ceremonial centres and 'converted' them to Christianity.

This was done with the full approval of the Church authorities in Rome. In the year 601, Pope Gregory I instructed Saint Augustine, whom he was sending on a mission to Britain, that the idols should be smashed but that the temples themselves 'should be sprinkled with holy water and altars set up in them in which relics are . . . enclosed. For we ought to take advantage of well-built temples by purifying them from devil worship and dedicating them to the service of the true God'.

The Pope believed that by these methods, the inhabitants of Britain would be encouraged to abandon their old deities and, even if they continued to use the ancient places of worship, would come to revere Christianity.

Thus, many of the old henges and stone circles became the settings for new churches and the earthen banks or rings of stones served to outline new sacred enclosures. At Ysbyty Cynfyn, some twelve miles east of Aberystwyth, five large upright stones, all that remains of a circle, can still be seen embedded in the wall which encloses the churchyard.

At St Tysilio's church, in Llandysiliogogo, something similar must have happened. There, in the modern churchyard, the circular shape of the old enclosure is still traceable, whilst just outside it, on the sloping side of the valley which leads to the sea, the spring which was used in the Bronze Age, and later by medieval pilgrims, still trickles from its hollow.

In the 1890s, when maintenance work was being carried out inside the church, a huge monolith was discovered buried beneath the pulpit. It was too large to remove and lies there still, out of sight, symbolically trodden beneath the feet of the Christian priesthood.

Other stones were 'Christianised' by the carving of crosses upon their sides. In the churchyard at Bridell, on the Pembrokeshire-Cardiganshire border, there remains a standing stone which has a Celtic cross cut upon one of its faces. There is also an Ogham inscription which reads 'NATTASAGRU MAQI MUCOI BRECI, (the stone) of Nettasagrus, son of the descendent of Brecos'.

A few miles westwards, at Nevern, the famous Vitelianus stone can be seen; this pillar, which commemorates a Romano-

Several large megaliths are embedded in the
churchyard wall at Ysbyty Cynfyn.

Maen Dewi, which was once used to build a house.

British citizen, may originally have been a Bronze Age maenhir.

As the centuries flowed by and the era of the standing stones receded into the darkness of the past, the maenhirs themselves became the victims of time. Many were destroyed in the 18th and 19th centuries when farmers, anxious to improve their lands, removed them. There are numerous instances of stones which were dynamited for this reason, and as recently as 1914, a complete circle in Carmarthenshire was destroyed by a farmer who dragged the stones away in order to grow crops in the field in which they stood.[5]

Other maenhirs were broken up and used for building purposes. One which almost suffered this fate was Maen Dewi, a stone near St. Davids which was once incorporated whole and undamaged into the wall of a *tŷ-un-nos* or 'overnight house' built in the early 19th century. The stone can now be seen behind Drws Gobaith cottage, on Dowrog Common, with the foundations of the earlier building still around it.

One maenhir which has entirely vanished from its place on a hill at Cefn Eithin farm, near Llandeilo, is Maen Llwyd. This 8ft 6ins high pillar, incised with the outline of a bow and arrow—which may in fact be an unfinished cross—was removed not because it stood in the way of agricultural improvements, but because it had for many years been leaning over and was in imminent danger of falling. In 1932, Maen Llwyd was given by the farm owner to the Carmarthen Antiquarian Society who, to preserve the stone from damage, removed it by lorry to the precincts of their musuem.

An unusual fate was reserved for the stone known as the Bryn Llewellyn maenhir. After lying recumbent for many years in the fields of Bryn Llewellyn farm, it was hauled by the owner of the farm, a Mr David Evans, to the burial ground of Capel Nenog in the village of Llidiadnennog. There it was laid upon the site of the grave he was eventually to occupy, where it can still be seen, inscribed with his name and farm.

Countless other stones, their original purpose dimly remembered, misunderstood or even forgotten, became the source of a rich tradition of folklore and legend. That heritage forms the subject of the next chapter of this book.

NOTES

[1] Ronald Hutton, *The Pagan Religions of the Ancient British Isles*, p. 132-138.

[2] John Evans, *The Environment of Early Man in the British Isles*, p. 91-113.

[3] ibid., p. 91-113.

[4] Ronald Hutton, *The Pagan Religions of the Ancient British Isles*, p. 136.

[5] R.C.A.M. *Inventory of County of Carmarthen*, p. 101.

7 TRADITIONS AND FOLKLORE

The origins of many of the legends connected with standing stones are almost as ancient as the stones themselves. The *Ladi Wen*, or White Lady, a ghostly figure who haunts many historic sites in Britain, may well be a distorted memory of the female deities who were once believed to be earth goddesses or to have ruled the underworld.

Several maenhirs in West Wales are said to be haunted by a White Lady. Perhaps the best known example is the horrific figure which is believed to lurk around the stones of Parc y Meirw. This spectre is usually seen at night, flitting between the pillars that loom above the sunken roadway leading across Mynydd Llanllawern. During the last century, any traveller using this route ran the risk of being pursued by the White Lady, who was likely to leap upon his back out of the darkness and tear him with her talons.[1] So feared was she, that after night-fall the local people used a much longer trackway across the mountain, which enabled them to give the stones a wide berth.

A much kinder and more helpful female spirit haunts the vicinity of a fallen maenhir at Lady's Gate near Strumble Head, some three or four miles west of Fishguard. This ghost is also dressed in white but is traditionally said to be either looking for a great treasure which is hidden nearby, or is waiting to reveal its location to anyone who comes in search of it.[2]

Another treasure lay hidden in the vicinity of Caerfarchell, to the east of St. Davids; according to a local tradition, there once existed near the hamlet a row of standing stones, at the end of which was buried a cache of gold. It is interesting to note that Caerfarchell is close to the route of the Bronze Age trackway known as the Golden Road (also Via Flamanda) and that during the age of the maenhirs gold was imported into Britain along this road from its source in the Wicklow Hills of Ireland.

Another ancient tradition which may lie behind the naming of a now vanished maenhir known as Llech yr Ochain, or Stone of Lamentation, in Cardiganshire, is the tale of the lost land of Cantre'r Gwaelod. This rich and fertile plain lay in what is now Cardigan Bay, its lush farmlands and sixteen noble cities protected from the sea by a system of embankments and sluice gates. The keeper of the sluice gates was Seithenyn, who in a drunken stupor, one night forgot to close the gates; the sea rolled mercilessly in and Cantre'r Gwaelod was lost.

The survivors of the inundation took refuge on the hills along what is now the west coast of Wales. The places in which they gathered to weep and look back over their drowned homes are still known by the names they were given then; Carn Ochain, the Mound of Sighs, and Trwyn yr Wylfa, the Point of the Sorrowful Hill.[3] Llech yr Ochain may well have marked one of these places, for it stood on a ridge above the brook which runs down to Traeth Penbryn, a mile or so east of Aberporth.

A few miles south-west of Fishguard is the Ffynnon Drudion standing stone, which was once, because of its name, believed to have been associated with the Druids. However, the Welsh word for Druid is Derwydd, whilst Drudion means heroes or brave men.[4] Possibly this stone is one which was once used to commemorate some now forgotten heroes; perhaps, after a battle, they drank from the nearby spring which bears their name, Ffynnon Drudion, the Spring of Heroes.

Saints and holy men also have their part to play in the folklore of standing stones. This is not surprising, considering the impact they made on Wales during the Dark Ages some 1,500 years ago, and the influence they had wielded over the minds of the people since then.

St. Samson, of whom many legends are told, was born in Dyfed of noble parentage and later became Abbot of Caldey, Abbot of Dol in Brittany, and Archbishop of York. He is commemorated in West Wales at many places which bear his name; these include farms, cross-roads, megalithic burial

The Ffynnon Drudion stone stands close to the
spring of the same name.

chambers, geographical features and a surprising number of maenhirs.

Samson is said to have played quoits with at least two standing stones in Cardiganshire (see Gazetteer). Both of these are, as a result, called Carreg Samson.

A third Carreg Samson, in the parish of Llanfihangel Ystrad, is supposed to have been marked by the saint's hands when he threw it down, presumably after carrying it for a great distance. The stone now lies in the bed of the Nant y Caer stream, having been dynamited many years ago.

Yet another Carreg Samson, near Croesffordd Rhydygolwg, south-east of Aberystwyth, is said to have stuck in the saint's shoe whilst he was out ploughing. He shook it out and threw it to the side of the field, where it has remained ever since. This stone, which is probably a boulder, not a standing stone, is also known as Y Garreg Wen (the White Rock). A store of treasure is said to be hidden beneath it, but if the stone is moved, thunder and lightning will break out. This type of story, involving elemental disturbances as a result of interference by people, is told of many genuine standing stones across the British Isles.[5]

It may also be worth mentioning that in another legend, Samson was one day threshing corn on Pendinas Hill across the valley from Llanbadarn Church, when the flail broke. The longer part flew across and fell in the churchyard; in his anger Samson threw the smaller part after it. Both pieces were later used to make the intricately-carved standing crosses which can now be seen inside the church.

The Devil also appears in a number of stories connected with standing stones, most notably in the tale of the three dancing stones of Stackpole. These have already been mentioned in Chapter 4 and consist of three maenhirs close to the village of Bosherston, south of Pembroke; two of the stones are known as the Devil's Quoit, whilst the third, now named the Harold Stone, was, during the last century, also known as the Devil's Quoit.

These three stones are said to leave their places on one night in the year when they go down to a spot variously known as Saice's, Sayce's or Saxon's Ford.[6] A coven of witches dances to the music of a flute which is played by the Devil as he sits on top of one of the stones. Anyone who witnesses this scene will enjoy great good luck during the following year.

The date of this annual performance is said by some people to be Midsummer's Eve, by others to be the 29th December.

The Devil is also reputed to be responsible for the location of the boulder known as Carreg y Big, which is to be found on high ground near Cross Inn in Cardiganshire and which may not be a standing stone at all. It is named because of its pointed or peaked top and in thick mist is said to resemble a huge figure wrapped in a grey cloak.

The stone was carried by the Devil from the top of Trichrug Mountain. He intended to use it in the building of Devil's Bridge in north Cardiganshire, but finding the stone to be extremely heavy, he sat down to rest. Suddenly, a cock began to crow, heralding the dawn and the Devil flew away, leaving the stone behind. It has remained on that spot ever since, with the marks of the Devil's finger-prints still on it.[7]

The Lady Stone on the roadside near Dinas, east of Fishguard, is also best seen on a misty day. It is then said to resemble a woman wearing a long hooded grey cloak. In the early half of the nineteenth century, when the mail coach ran regularly through Dinas from Cardigan to Fishguard, the outside passengers would doff their caps and bow as they rumbled past, such was the respect in which the stone was held.[8]

Other stones are associated with heroes or villains; Carreg Fyrddin, to the south of the A40 below Merlin's Hill, outside Abergwili, is named after Merlin, the great Arthurian wizard. He is said to have prophesied that a raven would one day drink a man's blood from the hollow at the top of the stone. Many hundreds of years later, possibly in the 18th century, a man hunting for treasure which he believed to be hidden beneath it, began digging away the earth on one side of the stone. Deeper and deeper he delved until suddenly Carreg Fyrddin toppled over and crushed him. A raven flapped down and pecked at the blood which splattered the stone.[9]

The maenhir was later restored to its original position by the owner of the farm where it now stands. According to tradition it

Carreg Fyrddin, the subject of a prophecy by
Merlin.

took the efforts of five horses pulling with strong chains to achieve this.

King Arthur is associated with a number of standing stones in West Wales. The most famous of these Arthurian connections is to be found in 'Y Mabinogi', a collection of tales written down in the 13th century, but derived from a much more ancient oral tradition.

This particular story concerns the efforts of Culhwch, a cousin of King Arthur, to win the hand of Olwen in marriage; her father, the giant Ysbaddaden, had agreed to the match only on condition that Culhwch should carry out a number of near-impossible tasks. Amongst the labours laid upon Culhwch was the seizure of a comb, a razor and a pair of shears which were carried between the ears of Twrch Trwyth; this boar, huge and evil-tempered, dwelt in Ireland and could only be hunted by an assembly of great heroes and huntsmen. Having, after great difficulty, persuaded the huntsmen to join him, Culhwch combined forces with King Arthur and many of his knights and together they set sail for Ireland. There they pursued Twrch Trwyth up an down the country, until at last he leaped into the sea to escape them. Followed by his sons, seven young pigs, the boar swam towards Wales and eventually came ashore at Porth Clais, near St. Davids.

Culhwch, King Arthur and their company continued the pursuit of the boar across the countryside of North Pembrokeshire. At Nevern, Twrch Trwyth turned and was driven southwards over the Presely Hills. At Cwm Cerwyn, where the hills enclose a bowl-shaped valley, the boar stood at bay. A terrible battle was fought, during which eight of King Arthur's greatest champions were slain; Gwarthegydd, son of Caw, Tarawg of Allt Clwyd; Rheiddwn son of Eli Adfer; Isgofan the Generous; Garselit the Irishman; Glaw son of Ysgawd; Isgawyn son of Banon; and Gwydre son of Arthur.

Eventually, after more fighting, Twrch Trwyth was chased into Cornwall and escaped only by leaping into the sea and swimming away. The comb, razor and shears were, however, wrested from him, and after fulfilling the other tasks Culhwch was able to marry his Olwen.

At Cwm Cerwyn, two stones were erected by King Arthur in memory of the warriors who had fallen. They stand there to this day and are known as Cerrig Meibion Arthur, the Stones of the Sons of Arthur.

Coitan Arthur is another stone with Arthurian connections. It is to be found in the bed of the Sawdde Fechan stream at Pont-yr-Aber, where it came to rest after being thrown by the king from the top of Pen Arthur Isa, a mile away. [10]

An outlaw named Morris, or Morus, is reputedly buried beneath the stone known as Bedd Morus (Morus's Grave) on Newport Mountain. Many years ago he lived in a cave somewhere on the slopes of the hill and would regularly issue forth to rob travellers using the trackway between Newport and the Gwaun Valley. He owned a little white dog which he had trained to recover the arrows he fired during the attacks. Eventually, the local inhabitants decided to put an end to his exploits; banding together, they marched in a body up to his cave and, after a short seige, burst in and captured him. He and his white dog were dragged down to the road way, where they were both killed and buried in a pit, over which a tall maenhir was erected. [11]

There is an alternative legend to this; Morus was not an outlaw, but was one of two young men who had both fallen in love with the daughter of the owner of Pontfaen House. She could not, or would not, choose between them. The two men fought a duel to decide who should marry her and the loser was buried beneath the stone, which ever since has been haunted by his ghost.

During the 17th or 18th century, a man called Davy Martin (Martin Davy in some versions), stole a sheep from Haverfordwest market and set off towards his home near Broad Haven. Instead of driving the sheep before him, Davy decided to carry it on his shoulders with the legs tied together on his chest. After a while, he became tired and sat down to rest with his back against a small standing stone. He pushed up his burden so that it lay on the top of the stone. Unfortunately the sheep began to struggle and slipped backwards, so that the rope binding its feet tightened around Davy's throat and throttled him. Ever since, the stone has been known as Martin Davy's stone, or the Hangstone Davy. It is still to be seen in the hedge on the left-hand side of the B4341 road leading from Haverfordwest to Broad Haven. [12]

Some stones are linked with real characters or actual historical events. Just outside the gates of Abermarlais Park, and almost on the verge of the Llandeilo-Llandovery road, stands the huge maenhir which was once known as Maen Cilan, but which is recorded on Ordnance Survey maps as Carreg Fawr. It is traditionally said to have been placed within the boundaries of the Park over five centuries ago by Sir Rhys ap Thomas, in commemoration of the Battle of Bosworth. If this is so, then presumably he ordered its removal from its original site; it was, however moved again in 1840 to its present place.[13]

A long and complicated story surrounds the stone known as St. Paul's Marble, which stands near Cilgwyn House, several miles south-west of Llandovery. This maenhir was originally situated near the farm of Pentwyn, the earlier name of which was Gelli Maen. The stone was at that time known as Y Sythfaen, the erect stone, and is said to have been surrounded by a hedge which had been specially planted to protect it. In 1825, Mr Holford, the owner of Cilgwyn, decided to remove the stone to a spot nearer his house. This task was carried out during his absence by his son, who succeeded only through the efforts of a large number of helpers and a team of twenty-five horses.

When the maenhir was re-erected on its new site, an inscription was placed upon it which read:

St. Paul's Marble
From Pentwyn Farm
Property of
J.J. Holford Esq.
Placed here
10th March 1825
by J.J.H. jun'r.

That, however, was not the only inscription which the boulder bore; another one was said to have been discovered, either on the maenhir itself, or on a stone some 18 inches long which had been buried at the foot of the larger stone. This legend stated, in poor and inaccurate Welsh:

St. Paul a Bregethodd
un y van hon/hyd flwdd
an a.d. LXVIII
Ag Elim ap Owen Goch
a laddwyd ag g(1)addwyd un man
o acos precthy Crist + 1604.

Translated roughly, this meant:

St. Paul preached
in this place up to
the year LXVIII
and Elim ap Owen Goch
was killed and buried in the same place
on account of preaching Christ + 1604

This second inscription has been regarded ever since as a hoax, perpetrated by Mr Holford junior, following the removal of the maenhir to its new site. There is no trace of any other inscription on the stone today, except the one recording its re-erection; nothing is known either of the whereabouts of the second, smaller stone which may have borne the lettering, or of the gold ornaments which were said to have been discovered under the larger maenhir when it was moved and which were supposed to have been sent to the British Museum.[14]

The Royal Commission for Ancient Monuments, in the survey of Carmarthenshire antiquities, suggests that Mr Holford junior may have developed the idea of linking his stone with St. Paul through his knowledge of the real inscribed stone of Paulinus, which once stood in the vicinity of Pentwyn. He was no doubt also aware of the many legends and stories which were told in Carmarthenshire of Owain Goch, or Owain Lawgoch, the Welsh hero who had rebelled against Edward III. Owain is said to have had a sister named Elin (not Elim), though nothing is known of her. If it was she who was mentioned in the inscription—and 'ap' usually denotes 'son of', not 'daughter or sister of'—then she presumably died centuries before the supposed martyrdom in 1604.

Owain Lawgoch was a great nephew of Llywelyn ap Gruffudd, Prince of Wales; following his revolt against the English king, he was murdered in France in 1378. In the years which followed, his reputation grew and he became an almost legendary figure.

In the popular imagination, he may have become confused with a much earlier hero with a similar name, Owain Goch, who lived and fought in Carmarthenshire centuries before Lawgoch. Nothing is now remembered of this warrior, except that he lies buried in a cave near Llandybïe.

Whatever the truth of the stories surrounding St. Paul's Marble, the real Owen Lawgoch, Owen ap Thomas ap Rhodri, has as his memorial an entirely different stone. Y Garreg Wen, the White Stone, is a small maenhir which is said to have been erected in his memory in a meadow known as Cwm Castell in the parish of Newchurch. Some time later, it was removed from that spot and was placed in the farmyard of Trawsmawr House.[15]

The stone with the longest record is probably Hirfaen Gwyddog, the huge monolith which stands on the boundary between the old counties of Cardigan and Carmarthen, a few miles south-east of Lampeter; it also marks the spot where three farms meet.

The stone is first mentioned in an entry written probably in the 10th century upon the margin of one of the pages of the 8th century gospels known as the Book of St. Chad. The volume belonged to the Church of Llandaff, to which a gift of land had been presented. One of the boundaries was noted as being 'behet hirmain guidauc' or 'as far as hirfaen gwyddog'. Mention of the maenhir occurs again in the 12th century, in the foundation charter of Talley Abbey, when in all probability the lands granted to it were the same as those once donated to Llandaff. In later confirmations of the Abbey lands made in 1324 and 1332, the name of the stone is given as 'Hyrvayn gudauc'.[16]

A manorial presentment of 1633 gives the boundaries of its lands as stretching from Llanlas to 'A stone called Hirvaen gwyddog gydant'.

Some sixty years later, in 1698, Edward Lhuyd noted in *Parochialia* that it was a 'large stone called Hyrvaun within a mile and a half of ye church; it is pitched on end in ye ground and about 4 yards long'.

It is not surprising that Hirfaen Gwyddog should have become such a landmark for it is truly impressive. It is 15 feet high and measures almost fourteen feet in circumference; each of its faces in mid-height is about 3ft 6ins wide.

By the 19th century the stone had become something of a tourist attraction. On 17th August 1861, a group of people started out from Lampeter 'to examine some of the antiquities in the vale of Teivy (*sic*). One of the antiquities was an enormous erect stone . . . still called by pre-eminence Hir Faen, the long or tall stone; and it merits its name, being about 16 feet in height'.

Hirfaen Gwyddog has the longest recorded history of any standing stone in Dyfed.

51

The Hirfaen stood at that time on the intersection of two boundary walls (there are 3 today). The unknown writer who described the visit in a letter to *Archaeologia Cambrensis* also expressed his surprise that the maenhir had been allowed to remain, for 'Cardiganshire landlords seem to care little for antiquities, and their agents know nothing about them'. The writer adds that 'the time may come as people get better informed when it will be thought an honour to have early British remains undisturbed on an estate; and when a landowner will be better pleased to have a carnedd lying untouched on his ground than to boast that he obtained from it so many coartloads of stone for the adjacent wall'.

The writer of this letter would no doubt have been horrified by two acts of vandalism perpetrated on the stone; at some time before his visit, the name 'I. Singer' was carved upon it, and thirteen years after that summer outing, a student from St. David's College, Lampeter, inscribed upon one of the stone's faces the following, 'S.D.C. Nov 5 1874 Dies Irae'.

The writer's complaint concerning the destruction of so many antiquities would still be justified today; in the years since 1861, as this book has already described, other stones have been damaged or destroyed.

It is not only the physical destruction which matters; a fund of ancient traditions and legends concerning the maenhirs has gone too. What stories lay behind the naming of stones such as Llech yr Ast, the Stone of the Bitch, or Cerrig yr Ŵyn, the Stones of the Lamb? What of Carreg y Bwci, the Stone of the Goblin, haunted by a ghost clad in white garments? Why is Llech yr Halen, the Pillar of Salt, also known as Llech yr Aberth, the Stone of Sacrifice?

We shall probably never know, for those tales were not written down and were lost with the passing of the generations which remembered and valued the old oral traditions of the countryside.

Only the stones remain and their numbers slowly dwindle. They are the powerful and enigmatic memorials to a vanished way of life and to a forgotten people.

NOTES

[1] *Archaeologia Cambrensis* 1868, p. 177.
[2] Richard Fenton, *Historical Tour through Pembrokeshire*, p. 16.
[3] *Pembrokeshire Antiquities*, p. 22.
[4] *RCAM Inventory for Pembroke*, p. 177.
[5] Chris Barber, *More Mysterious Wales*, p. 1.
[6] Richard Fenton, *Historical Tour through Pembrokeshire*, p. 228.
[7] Chris Barber, *More Mysterious Wales*, p. 5.
[8] *RCAM, Inventory for Pembroke*, p. 99.
[9] *Archaeologia Cambrensis* 1876, p. 236.
[10] *Archaeologia Cambrensis* 1874, p. 89.
[11] *Archaeologia Cambrensis* 1875, p. 305.
[12] *Archaeologia Cambrensis* 1872, p. 139.
[13] *RCAM, Inventory for Carmarthen*, p. 182.
[14] *RCAM, Inventory for Carmarthen*, p. 217.
[15] *RCAM, Inventory for Carmarthen*, p. 221.
[16] *RCAM, Inventory for Carmarthen*, p. 208.

APPENDIX: THE EXCAVATIONS

The Devil's Quoit Standing Stone, Stackpole warren.

This stone proved, upon excavation, to occupy a site with a long history of use. One of the first features to have been built, possibly at about 1,300-1,400 B.C., was a round hut with a porch. The internal walls of the hut contained two scooped-out areas which the excavators suggested were cupboards. The function of the building was uncertain; it might have been a dwelling associated with a nearby cultivated area, but a few fragments of burnt human bone were discovered in the interior and therefore it could have been used at some point for ritual purposes. The structure had finally been destroyed by fire.

In the years following the fire, a layer of soil developed over the site which, in turn, had been covered by deposits of wind-blown sand. Two pits were subsequently dug nearby, before the raising of the standing stone; this took place roughly between 1,400 B.C., the date of the hut, and 940 B.C., when a cremation burial was placed in a pit near the stone.

A number of burials were found in the general area surrounding the stone, but these took place at a much later date, during the Iron Age. Most were of children, and one of a crouched adult on the eastern side of the setting was radio-carbon dated to around 1,400 B.C. The upper levels of the site contained the remains of huts from the Iron Age or the Romano-British period.

The excavation did reveal, however, that during the Bronze Age the Devil's Quoit had been only one element in a fascinating and complex site. Over 3,000 other stones were discovered; all were quite small and appeared to have been arranged in upright rows to form a trapezoidal shape extending roughly north-eastwards away from the maenhir. The west end of this area, where the quoit stood, was rounded, whilst in the centre of the setting a large timber post had once been erected. On the south-western side an alignment of upright, water-worn stones led away from the site.

The careful arrangements of so many small stones near a maenhir is not unique to the Devil's Quoit, nor are cobbled areas to Rhos y Clegyrn. At other sites in Wales, and across Britain, rows of tiny upright stones have been found carpeting the areas around standing stones. These settings are often arranged into boat or 'D' shapes, or into parallel straight lines; sometimes the rows open out into fan shapes. Their exact function, like so much else from the Bronze Age, is uncertain. [1]

St. Ishmael's

Another Pembrokeshire stone, near St. Ishmael's, was excavated in the early 1980s; like the others, it was revealed to be part of a complex and long-used site. A number of pits were discovered, all dug during the Bronze Age, one of which had held the original standing stone. The others may also have held stones or wooden posts, though in two of them, cremations had been deposited. Several of the pits, including the socket hole of the stone, had been cut into earlier pits.

The most curious feature of the site lay towards the centre of the complex, where a circular trench was discovered. It was packed with boulders which appeared to have been brought from a beach—there is an inlet of the sea several hundred yards away. This trench bore on its inner and outer edges traces of upright poles, whilst along the middle a number of wooden stakes seem to have been set. It is possible that some sort of round hut or similar structure had once stood there, but any further clues had been destroyed by ploughing.

There was evidence of another circular building located to the south of the first structure, where a second, smaller circle of possible stake holes was discovered. [2]

Parc Maen

A round house may also have stood adjacent to a group of standing stones at Parc Maen, near Llangolman, in the Presely Hills. Excavations were carried out here in the 1980s and a large number of post holes were discovered. One group of these may have been arranged into a circle, but it was impossible to be sure, as the pits had been damaged by ploughing. Other pits were filled with charcoal, which proved, upon analysis, to have come from oak wood.

Two standing stones remained upright on the site, but five others had fallen and two of these seemed to have been dynamited as part of land clearances earlier this century. The remains were still lying half buried in the soil.

The site also included a cairn, which may have at one time contained cremations, and there was some evidence of a burial in one of the nearby pits. To the east of the cairn was a large spread of charcoal-rich soil, across which lay scattered many small stones, 60% of which were quartz; they may well have been deliberately deposited there when the site was in use, perhaps to mark out a special area, perhaps for some other reason not now understood.

Aber Camddwr

The excavations at this site, situated in the Pumlumon range of hills, east of Cardigan Bay, were carried out in the early 1980s, when the waters of the Nant-y-Moch reservoir were lowered to allow maintenance work on the dam to be undertaken.

The main feature of the site was again a cairn; it had an unusual porch-like annexe to one side, where two upright pillars marked what may have been a temporary entrance.

A number of standing stones had been raised close to and in the vicinity of the cairn. Some of these had been placed in pits which may first have held wooden stakes, whilst one stone stood in a hole containing a filling of charcoal, in which was found a fragment of bone. On the south side of the cairn was an alignment of three stones running south-west to north-east, and a short distance away was a group of sandstone pillars which might once have formed a circle. Over 100 stake holes were also discovered, but they formed no discernible pattern.

NOTES

[1] Current Archaeology No. 82, p. 28-32.
[2] *Archaeologia Cambrensis* 1989.

GAZETTEER OF SITES

The following gazetteer of selected sites has been arranged using the old county names which existed before these areas were absorbed into the 'new' county of Dyfed in the 1970s. Dyfed will shortly cease to exist and Pembrokeshire, at least, is likely to be re-established; I have assumed for the purposes of this book that Cardiganshire and Carmarthenshire will also re-appear.

The locations of the sites are given by a six figure grid reference. The problem of which stones to include and which to omit has not been an easy one; I have made the selection on the grounds that a maenhir is of particular interest, that it has been mentioned in the text, or that access to it is reasonably easy.

Most of the maenhirs are to be found on private land. It is advisable, whenever possible, to contact the landowner for permission to visit them.

The stones mentioned in this text are marked with an asterisk.

The following 1:50 000 scale Ordnance Survey maps have been used in compiling this gazetteer: Sheet 135 Aberystwyth; Sheet 145 Cardigan; Sheet 146 Lampeter and Llandovery; Sheet 157 St David's and Haverfordwest; Sheet 158 Tenby; Sheet 159 Swansea and Gower.

Cardiganshire
*Aber Camddwr
SN 761 869
> Excavated in the 1980s, the site has been flooded again following completion of repairs to the Nant-y-Moch dam. The cairn was re-constructed beside the reservoir.

Bron Caradog
SN 694 702

Bryn y Maen
SN 633 573

*Buwch a'r Llo (Cow and Calf)
SN 722 833
> These two stones are spectacularly sited on the borders of a coniferous plantation, with rolling moorlands and hills stretching away in all directions. A third stone is to be found by the roadside where it enters the plantation (see Mynydd March).

Carreg Fawr
SN 308 530

Carreg Lwyd
SN 307 529
> Both Carreg Fawr and Carreg Lwyd stand on the sides of a small valley sloping down to the sea, north-east of Morfa Ganol Farm.

*Carreg Samson
SN 726 712
> One of the stones with which St. Samson used to play quoits. Situated 70 yards east of the ford through Nant Cil Meddu and to the south of the lane leading to Cilmeddu Farm from the Methodist chapel of Ysbyty Ystwyth.

*Carreg Samson
SN 741 703
> Another of St. Samson's quoits, to be found in the field to the north-east of Llethr Farm.

*Carreg Samson
SN 518 562
> There is a tradition that St. Samson threw it down and left the marks of his hands on it. It was blasted with dynamite some years ago, and now lies in the bed of the Nant-y-Gaer stream.

*Cerrig-yr-Ŵyn (Stones of the Lamb)
SN 685 837

Court Grange Mine Maenhir
SN 661 856
> A stone consisting of white quartz, it has been moved to Penrhyn-coch, (SN 643 842) where, mounted on a plinth, and marked with a cross, it serves as a war memorial.

Esgair Hir Mine
SN 729 908

Llech Gron
SN 542 648

*Llech-yr-Ast (Stone of the Bitch)
SN 222 484
> Two stones which may be the remains of a cromlech.

Maen Gwyn
SN 686 688
> This stone was blown up in 1939; its remains were used as gate posts on the adjacent road.

Maen Gwyn
SN 382 433

Mynydd March
SN 721 834
>Situated close to the Buwch a'r Llo stones.

Nant Glandŵr
SN 730 830

Nant y Maen
SN 761 583

Noyadd Trefawr
SN 258 463
>The remains of a henge or embanked circle.

Pant Garreg Hir
SN 704 835
>Stands on the lawn in front of a farmhouse overlooking Cwm Symlog.

Pen y Castell
SN 691 848

Pen Maen Gwyn
SN 752 650

Plas Gogerddan
SN 626 835
>A row of 3 stones once stood here, now only 2 remain. Excavations were carried out in 1986. To the north of the stones a pit containing carbonised grain was discovered, though this may have belonged to an earlier settlement on the site. Other pits lay nearby, one of which held a cremation burial. An empty burial cist was also uncovered, but the most interesting feature of the site was an alignment of 3 massive post holes running north to south.

St. Michael's
SN 235 485

*St. Tysilio's Church, Llandysiliogogo
SN 364 575
>The circular shape of the old sacred enclosure is still traceable in the modern, extended churchyard, especially where the wall follows the ancient boundary to the north and west. In the field immediately to the north, just beyond the limits of the churchyard, the ancient spring still issues from a hollow in the ground. This was a healing well in medieval times and is still encircled by trees.

*Ysbyty Cynfyn circle
SN 752 791
>The circular churchyard is bounded by a wall into which are set five large monoliths, all that remains of a circle of stones.

Carmarthenshire
*Abermarlais
SN 694 293

Banc Rhosgoch Fach
SN 435 541
>Two stones remain of a row of three. The site was excavated in the 1930s and again in 1989. Pits with charcoal fillings were discovered to the west of the setting.

Brynmaen
SN 554 067
>This maenhir is almost 15ft in height.

*Carreg Fawr Nant Jack
SN 357 109
>The Royal Commission for Ancient Monuments, in its inventory for Carmarthenshire, records that this stone measured some 66 inches in height, and could be found approximately 600 yards to the east of the village of Llanstephan, close to the landing place of the old ferry. In the mid 19th century it stood high and dry above the tide line, but by the 1920s it was covered by the incoming waters. To the east of it, 15ft away, was a smaller stone about 12 inches high.

Carreg Fyrddin
SN 459 211
>Located in a field called Parc y maen llwyd, this stone is visible from the A40.

*Carreg Wen
SN 375 242

*Carreg y Bwci
SN 646 321
>The name translates as 'the Goblin's Stone'; although it is sometimes described as a fallen maenhir, or as the remains of a tomb, R.C.A.M. considered this to be a glacial erratic boulder.

*Cefn Cethin, Maen Llwyd
SN 637 191
>The grid reference given here is for the original site; the stone is now to be found in the grounds of the Museum at Abergwili, Carmarthen.

Cefn Gwenffrwd
SN 755 472
>This maenhir is said to be an ancient boundary stone which marks the junction of several mountain paths and the meeting of two or more manors. In the same area are to be found the remains of a stone circle and an alignment of stones; both of these sites are now covered by a forestry plantation.

*Coitan Arthur
SN 737 220
>In the bed of the Sawdde Fechan stream, near Pont Aber.

Clomendy Farm
SN 386 148

81 inches in height, this maenhir was also known as the Quoit Stone, or Merlin's Quoit. The Gilfach and Hendy stones (see below) are nearby.

*Ffos y Maen
SN 414 283

Ffynnon Iago
SN 548 426

Standing on land belonging to Capel Iago Farm, this pillar now measures some 30 inches in height, but the surrounding ground level is known to have been raised. During the medieval period a chapel dedicated to St. James is said to have been located nearby. There was also a spring known as Ffynnon Iago.

*Gilfach (and Hendy)
SN 383 145

Two stones separated by a narrow lane, in the fields of Gilfach and Hendy farms.

Gwynfaes
SN 785 409

Situated some 5 miles north of Llandovery, this pointed, triangular stone is 76 inches high and stands in a lane known as Sarn Ddu, 200 yards south-east of Gwynfaes farm.

Halfway House
SN 451 121

This 9 feet high maenhir was named after a nearby public house.

*Hirfaen Gwyddog
SN 624 464

The same manorial presentment of 1633 which describes the boundaries as including Hirfaen Gwyddog also goes on to say that the boundary stretches 'from thence unto another stone, called Byrfaen yr esceir berevedd' (sic.) This second maenhir, which was apparently about eight feet tall, has since disappeared; R.C.A.M. mentions a belief that it was buried in the latter half of the nineteenth century, during 'a perambulation of the county boundaries'.

Llandeilo Bridge
SN 626 217

Two stones which were omitted from the original R.C.A.M., inventory, drawn up in the 1920s. One maenhir can be seen about 250 yards south of the bridge and is 6 feet high; the second, 4 feet tall, is 250 yards south west of the bridge.

*Llanybydder
SN 549 395

An alignment of 18 stones on Mynydd Llanybydder, now lost in a forestry plantation.

*Llech Ciste
SN 514 261

The remains of a row of four stones.

*Llech yr Halen
SN 666 109

The name means 'Pillar of Salt'; also known as Llech yr Aberth (Arberth), or 'Stone of Sacrifice'. There is no explanation for either name.

Llechdwnny Stones
SN 431 101

Two stones on private land near the house of the same name; one can be found about 84ft to the south-east of the remains of a ruined cromlech, the second is some 400ft north of it.

Lletyʹrychen Farm
SN 463 019 and
SN 461 016

(Os map Lletyrychen) Two stones, one 55 inches in height, partly buried in a hedge, the other prostrate in a field known as Parc Maen Llwyd.

Maen Melyn
SN 347 127

Consisting of red sandstone, this maenhir measures 85 inches in height and 150 inches in width.

Maen Melyn
SN 131 252

*Meini Gwyn
SN 459 261

Meini Gŵyr
SN 141 265

The remains of an embanked circle, now situated behind a row of modern bungalows. The circle is a scheduled ancient monument, and access to it is gained through a wooden gate next to the last bungalow in the row. A pair of standing stones can be found in a field to the west. The circle was known as Buarth Arthur (Arthur's Cowshed).

*Mynydd
SN 735 447

Stands near an ancient trackway across Mynydd Mallaen; a second stone can be found some 600 yards to the north-west.

Mynydd Llangyndeyrn
SN 482 132

The 9ft high stone originally lay prostrate.

Excavated and re-erected in 1976, when evidence was discovered that a timber structure had once stood against the stone. A ring trench was also discovered nearby. A number of cairns and a second, smaller, standing stone had also been erected in the immediate vicinity during the Bronze Age.

Nantgaredig
SN 495 212

The two stones situated in the field to the rear of Station road used to be thought of as the remains of a cromlech. Recent excavation has revealed that the stones are, in fact, set into the entrance of an oval-shaped earthwork enclosure, some 250 feet across; this was surrounded by a ditch with an outer bank running around it. Much of the site has been built over in recent years.

Parc y Garreg, Glanrhyd Farm
SN 141 180

This 6ft high monolith was removed from the field in which it stood in about 1778, and forms the centre pier of a two-arch doorway at Glanrhyd farm building.

*St. Paul's Marble
SN 748 301

Sythfaen
SN 670 224

Although it now measures about 77 inches in height, this monolith has suffered damage in the past; it was once broken in two at a point 18 inches from the ground, but has been well mended.

Sythfaen Llwyn Du
SN 675 244

The weatherworn surface of this maenhir is said to bear the marks of carving.

Y Garreg Goch
SN 456 150

Stands in a hedge; about 200 yards away, in the middle of a field, there is a second stone. Other maenhirs, now destroyed, were once to be found in the vicinity. One of these was the Closteg stone, inscribed with a cross.

Pembrokeshire
*Bedd Morus (Morris)
SN 038 365

A recent inscription cut upon the stone records that it marks the junction of two parishes.

*Bridell
SN 176 421

*Budloy
SN 065 285

*Cerrig Meibion Arthur
SN 118 310

Cornel Bach
SN 082 279

Two maenhirs in a field beside a lane leading off the B4313 on the northern side of Maenclochog; they are more than 120 ft apart, a much wider separation than is usual with pairs of stones. These stones are not marked on all OS maps.

*Devil's Quoit
SR 963 964

One of the three dancing stones of Stackpole; it stands in a field near Sampson's Cross.

*Devil's Quoit, Stackpole Warren
SR 983 951

One of three Devil's Quoits in Pembrokeshire; also one of the three dancing stones of Stackpole. Recently excavated, this maenhir is not accessible to the public. Not shown on all OS maps.

*Ffynnon Drudion
SN 921 365

There are alternatives to the legend of the heroes who gave their name to the spring and the stone. Drudion may be a form of Tridian, the name of a local saint about whom little else is known. A neighbouring farm is known as Llandridian, the church or setlement of Dridian.

In 1326, however, the well was known as Fonnan Pedrykyaun and by 1588 it was called Fynnon Pendrigion. 'Pen' means 'head' or 'end' so the well may have marked the boundary of lands owned by a man called Drigion.

A third suggestion is that Drygion means bad or wicked persons and comes from 'drwg', bad or wicked.

Fragwyr-frân
SN 005 314

Situated in a field on the farm of the same name beside a minor road leading northwards out of the village of Puncheston.

*Gors Fawr Stone Circle
SN 135 294

On common land beside a minor road south of the village of Mynachlogddu; a few yards north of the circle are two fine maenhirs, the outliers mentioned in Chapter 4. The rocky outcrop of Carn Meini, the source of the Stonehenge blue-stones, is clearly visible further north.

*Hangstone Davy
SM 896 147

    In a hedge beside the B4341 Haverfordwest to Broad Haven road. It appears to be roughly carved with a cross. Some authorities doubt that this stone dates to the Bronze Age, but it has, in any case, been moved from its original position.

*Harold Stone, Broad Haven
SM 861 147

    Situated in the back garden of St. Catherine's bungalow overlooking St Bride's Bay, this 5ft 6ins high stone is said to be all that remains of a stone circle. Other maenhirs are to be seen embedded in the hedge near Upper Lodge (SM 861 143), further down the hill towards Broad Haven. These also were said to have been part of a circle. There is no record of two circles having stood in the vicinity, so either the Upper Lodge stones were dragged from the same ring which contained the Harold Stone and were used to build a hedge, or the Harold Stone stood outside, but was associated with, the circle.

*Harold Stone, Skomer Island
SR 734 096

*Harold Stone, Stackpole Farm
SR 968 959

    The third of the three dancing stones of Stackpole; also once known as the Devil's Quoit.

*Lady Stone
SM 996 376

    In a hedge beside the A487, on the left approaching Dinas from Fishguard.

*Lady's Gate Stone
SM 908 392

    Now fallen, this maenhir lies on private land.

Longstone, Amroth
SN 146 096

*Mabe's Gate Stone
SM 827 076

    About 320 yards south of Mabe's Gste Farm, in a field to the right of a minor road leading to Monk's Haven.

*Maen Dewi
SM 775 275

Parc Hen Stone
SM 932 390

Parc Lan
SN 090 358

    This pair of stones is unusual; they stand facing one another, instead of facing in the same direction, as is normal with pairs. There is no explanation for this feature.

*Parc Maen
SN 113 283

    The site of recent excavations mentioned in the text.

*Parc y Meirw
SM 998 359

Parc y Tywod
SN 088 278

*Rhos y Clegyrn
SM 913 355

*St. Ishmael's
SM 848 084

    One of the recently excavated stones mentioned in the text.

Tafarn y Bwlch
SN 082 337

    A pair of small stones on the moorland beside the B4329 Cardigan-Haverfordwest road. Another stone can be found beside the road at 081 332.

Trecenny Stone
SM 766 257

    A second stone is reputed to have stood close to the one which can now be seen in the field adjacent to the minor road leading past Trecenny Farm, St Davids.

*Tremaenhir Stones
SM 826 263

    Two stones, widely separated, at Tre-maenhir Farm, on a minor road from King-heriot and Middle Mill. One, a very shapely stone, bears the initials 'J.G'. These were cut by John Gibson, who was born at the farm and lived there for most of his life. There was a tradition in his family that, before the fields were enclosed, the farm had been a sheepwalk; the rounding-up of the flocks had taken place at three meini-hirion, which had given the farm its name, Tre-maenhir, or Tri-maen-hir. There is no trace now of the third stone, although it is said that a largish stone was built into the wall over the fireplace in one of the farm rooms.

Waun Lwyd
SN 158 312

    Two stones on private land near Mynachlogddu.

Waun Mawn Stone
SN 080 339

On moorland a few hundred yards to the west of the B4329, at Tafarn y Bwlch. A short distance away, at 084 340, are three stones, only one of which is erect; said to be the remains of a circle.

*Y Garreg Hir
SN 064 351

This fine maenhir stands beside an ancient trackway from Tafarn y Bwlch; the view over the Gwaun Valley is breathtaking.

BIBLIOGRAPHY

ARCHAEOLOGIA CAMBRENSIS.

ATKINSON, R.J.C., *Stonehenge; Archaeology and Interpretation* (Pelican, 1979).

BARBER, C. *More Mysterious Wales* (Paladin 1986).

BRADLEY, R. *The Social Foundations of Prehistoric Britain* (Longman 1984).

BRIARD, J. *The Bronze Age in Barbarian Europe* Book Club Associates 1979).

BURL, A. *Prehistoric Astonomy and Ritual* (Shire 1983).

BURL, A. *Rings of Stone* (Book Club Associates 1979).

BURL, A. *Rites of the Gods* (J.M. Dent & Sons 1981).

BURL, A. *The Stone Circles of the British Isles* (Yale University Press, 1976).

BURL, A. *From Carnac to Callanish* (Yale University Press, 1993).

CURRENT ARCHAEOLOGY

DAVIS, P. *Historic West Wales* (Christopher Davies 1992).

EVANS, J.G. *The Environment of Early Man in the British Isles* (Book Club Associates 1976).

FENTON, R. *Historical Tour through Pembrokeshire* (Davies and Co. 1903).

GERALD OF WALES *The Journey through Wales; The description of Wales* (Penguin Classics 1978).

HADINGHAM, E. *Circles and Standing Stones* (Abacus 1978).

HADINGHAM. E. *Early Man and the Cosmos* (Heinemann 1983).

HEDGES, J.G. *Tomb of the Eagles* (John Murray 1984).

HILLS, C. *The Blood of the British* (Guild Publishing 1986).

HUTTON, R. *The Pagan Religions of the Ancient British Isles* (Basil Blackwell 1991).

JONES, F. *The Holy Wells of Wales* (University of Wales 1954).

LEWIS, J.M. *The Standing Stones of Pembrokeshire* (Pembrokeshire Historian No.2, 1966).

MACKIE, E. *The Megalith Builders* (Phaidon, 1977).

MERRIFIELD, R. *The Archaeology of Ritual and Magic* (Batsford 1987).

PEMBROKESHIRE ANTIQUITIES (Solva 1897).

PEMBROKESHIRE ARCHAEOLOGICAL (Tenby, John Leach 1908).

RACKHAM, O. *The History of the Countryside* (J.M. Dent and Sons 1986).

R.C.A.M. *Inventory for the County of Carmarthen* H.M.S.O. 1917).

R.C.A.M. *Inventory for the County of Pembroke* (H.M.S.O. 1925)

WAINWRIGHT, G. *The Henge Monuments; Ceremony and Society in Prehistoric Britain* (Thames and Hudson 1989).

WOOD, J.E. *Sun, Moon and Standing Stones* (Oxford University Press 1980).

INDEX